I0794498

A Sad Ant

by Natalie Lambert
illustrated by Donald Wu

Practice Decodable 10

Mc Graw Hill Education

Bothell, WA • Chicago, IL • Columbus, OH • New York, NY

MHEonline.com

Send all inquiries to:
McGraw-Hill Education
8787 Orion Place
Columbus, OH 43240

ISBN: 978-0-02-146195-0
MHID: 0-02-146195-3

Printed in the United States of America.

7 8 9 CTM 23

A man sat and sat.

Ants stand on sand.

Ants see a man.

Can a man see ants?

A man can.

A sad ant sat.